HISTORY DETERMINES HERSTORY

JORI O'NEALE

Copyright © 2025 by Jori O'Neale
All rights reserved.

No part of this publication may be reproduced, stored in a retrieval system, or transmitted in any form or by any means—electronic, mechanical, photocopying, recording, or otherwise—without the prior written permission of the publisher, except in the case of brief quotations used in critical articles or reviews.

ISBN: 979-8-89741-017-0

Published by The 1 and Only Publishing
www.the1andonlypublishing.com
info@the1andonlypublishing.com

This book is registered with the United States Copyright Office. All rights are protected under Title 17 of the U.S. Code.

This is a work of nonfiction. Names and identifying details may have been changed to protect privacy. All testimonies and stories are shared with permission. The author and publisher make no claims to provide clinical, legal, or professional advice.

Scripture Acknowledgments

Scripture quotations taken from the **HOLY BIBLE, NEW INTERNATIONAL VERSION® (NIV®)**
Copyright © 1973, 1978, 1984 by International Bible Society. Used by permission of Zondervan. All rights reserved.

James 2:17 quoted from the **Amplified Bible**,
Copyright © 2015 by The Lockman Foundation. Used by permission. www.Lockman.org

Permissions & Disclosures

Written permissions are obtained (or pending) from **Aisha Oliver, Kristina Holloway, and Ebony Guerrier** for the inclusion of their stories and organizational affiliations.

Citation details for the **Crossroads Church article** (author, date, and source URL) are forthcoming.

Historical facts cited in the text are supported by academic sources. Full citations will appear in the Notes or References section.

All recommended reading includes current publishing information and ISBNs in the Resources section.

Any extended quotations from previously published works are used with permission or within fair use standards.

For rights, permissions, or bulk ordering inquiries, contact:
info@the1andonlypublishing.com

DEDICATION

It has been said that behind every great man is a great woman. While this may be true, Ron O'Neale, you and I both know you are the real MVP of this family. I know full well that God gave me you because He knew that I needed a strong leader to ensure that I stayed on the straight and narrow path. Your consistent love and support of all of my crazy endeavors has helped me not only reach for my goals, but actually realize them.

I was blessed with a partner in the gospel who helps me steward both our family and my gifts well. Your leadership speaks volumes through your service to our children, to your wife, and all those God places in your path. Our sons are blessed to have a role model such as yourself to learn from. I love you.

CONTENTS

FOREWORD 1
    Why This Book Matters 1
    How to Use This Book 1

A LETTER FROM THE AUTHOR 3

PART 1: UNDERSTANDING YOUR PAST 5

CHAPTER 1: UNDERSTANDING WHY WE DO WHAT WE DO 7
    What's Your Narrative? 7
    The Power of Upbringing 8
    The Impact of Words & Family Culture 10
    Turning Pain into Purpose 10
    Reflection Questions 11

CHAPTER 2: UNLIKELY CANDIDATES – WOMEN GOD USED 15
    Rahab: Faith in Unlikely Places 15
    Ruth: Loyalty & New Beginnings 17
    Mary Magdalene: From Brokenness to Boldness 18
    Martha Dandridge: A Legacy of Service 19
    Madam C.J. Walker: Turning Trials into Triumph 20
    Modern Reflection: Who Are the "Unlikely Candidates" Today? 21
    Reflection Questions 22

PART 2: OWNING YOUR PRESENT 27

CHAPTER 3: THE LORD DETERMINES HER PATH 29
    Dreams Deferred: Learning from Setbacks 29
    The Power of Determination 30
    When Preparation Meets Purpose 30

The Real Problem 31
Mental & Spiritual Preparation 31
The Habits That Got Me Here 31
Walking in Alignment, Not Just Ambition 32
Lessons from My Vendor Story 32
Moving Forward with Wisdom 33
Reflection Questions 34

CHAPTER 4: THE EFFECTS OF FAITH ON HERSTORY 37
Faith + Works: Why Both Matter 37
Modern Women of Faith — Living Testimonies 38
Turning Pain into Service 40
The Ripple Effect 40
Finding Your "Why" 41
Reflection Questions 42

PART 3: RENEWING YOUR MIND 47
CHAPTER 5: HER THOUGHTS DETERMINE HER STORY 49
The Power of Thought Patterns 49
The Formation of Mental Patterns 50
Identifying Limiting Beliefs 50
How These Beliefs Affect Our Lives 51
Practicing a New Identity in Christ 51
Daily Mental Renewal Practices 52
5. Community Accountability 53
Helping Others Do the Same 54
Reflection Questions 55

PART 4: EMBRACING YOUR LIFETIME ASSIGNMENT 59
CHAPTER 6: REASONS, SEASONS, AND A LIFETIME 61
Who's Driving Your Destiny? 61
The Comparison Trap 62

- Soul, Spirit, and Body — Aligning All Three 62
- Letting Go of Comparison 63
- Living for Legacy, Not Just Today 64
- Daily Choices, Eternal Impact 65
- Reflection Questions 66

PART 5: LIVING IT OUT 71
CHAPTER 7: FROM HERSTORY TO LEGACY 73
- Finding Meaning in Your Story 73
- Practical Ways to Serve Others 74
- Building Community & Sisterhood 76
- Passing Down a Faithful Legacy 77
- Reflection Questions 79

TOOLS & RESOURCES 83
- Week 1: Foundation Building 85
- Week 2: Examining Your Story 88

DAILY PRAYER PROMPTS 97
- Morning Prayers 97
- Evening Prayers 98

JOURNAL PAGE TEMPLATES 99
DAILY REFLECTION TEMPLATE 100
WEEKLY STORY REVIEW TEMPLATE 103
MONTHLY LEGACY ASSESSMENT 106
- Finding a Mentor 109
- Building Community 110
- Books for Continued Growth 111
- Online Communities 112

FINAL BLESSING & CALL TO ACTION 113
A PRAYER FOR YOU, SISTER 115
YOUR STORY MATTERS—SHARE IT 117
REMEMBER THIS TRUTH 119
ACKNOWLEDGMENTS 120
ABOUT THE AUTHOR 122

COMPREHENSIVE REFERENCE TABLE 125
    Biblical References 127
    Published Articles and Online Sources 134
    Historical Sources and Biographical Information 134
    Book and Resource Recommendations 136
    Additional References for Verification 137
    Notes for Complete Citation 138
    Bibliography Format for Academic/Professional Use 139

FOREWORD

WHY THIS BOOK MATTERS

Have you ever wondered why your life unfolded the way it did? Why certain painful experiences shaped your early years, or why specific struggles keep surfacing in your story?

This book was written for the woman who knows there's more to her story than the pain she's endured. It's for the sister who suspects God has a purpose for her past but isn't sure how to uncover it. Most importantly, it's for you—the woman ready to transform her history into a powerful testimony that changes not just her own life, but the lives of others.

HOW TO USE THIS BOOK

This isn't meant to be a quick read. It's designed as an interactive journey. Keep a journal and pen nearby as you read. Each chapter includes reflection questions that will help you process your own story through the lens of faith. Consider reading with a trusted friend or small group—some discoveries are meant to be shared.

Set aside quiet time for each chapter. Some sections may trigger difficult memories or emotions. That's okay—healing often requires us to revisit painful places with new eyes and God's grace.

Most importantly, approach this book with prayer. Ask God to reveal His heart for your story as you read.

A LETTER FROM THE AUTHOR

Dear Sister,

Your story has power.

I know it might not feel that way right now. Maybe your story feels more like a collection of painful chapters you'd rather forget. Perhaps you look at your past and see only mistakes, missed opportunities, or moments you wish you could rewrite.

But what if I told you that every chapter of your story—even the most painful ones—has been allowed by God for a specific purpose? What if the very experiences that brought you the most pain could become the source of your greatest ministry?

This isn't just wishful thinking or spiritual platitudes. This is the truth I've discovered through my own journey from brokenness to breakthrough, and it's the same truth countless women throughout history have proven true.

Your past doesn't have to define you, but it was never meant to be wasted either. God is in the business of taking our most broken pieces and creating something beautiful—not in spite of our pain, but because of how He transforms it.

In this book, we'll explore how your personal history fits into God's greater story. We'll examine the lives of women who faced impossible circumstances yet became conduits of God's grace. Most importantly, we'll discover practical ways to allow God to redeem every part of your story for His glory and the good of others.

This journey requires courage. It means looking honestly at your past, examining your present thought patterns, and stepping boldly into the future God has prepared for you. But I promise you this: on the other side of this process is a woman who knows her worth, understands her purpose, and walks confidently in her calling.

Your story matters. Your pain has purpose. Your faithfulness will be rewarded.

Let's discover how together.

With love and sisterhood,
Jori O'Neale

UNDERSTANDING YOUR PAST

CHAPTER 1:
UNDERSTANDING WHY WE DO WHAT WE DO

"Search me, God, and know my heart; test me and know my anxious thoughts. See if there is any offensive way in me, and lead me in the way everlasting."
— PSALM 139:23-24

WHAT'S YOUR NARRATIVE?

Close your eyes for a moment and imagine someone describing you to a mutual friend before you all meet. What words would they use? What characteristics would they highlight? How would they capture the essence of who you are?

Now, here's the deeper question: How do you think of yourself? What story do you tell yourself about who you are, what you're capable of, and what you deserve?

This internal narrative—the story we tell ourselves about ourselves—shapes everything. It influences how we handle stress, how we interact with others, our ability to give and receive love, and whether we believe we're worthy of good things.

But where does this narrative come from? The answer is both simple and complex: our history.

THE POWER OF UPBRINGING

When you hear the word "upbringing," what images come to mind? Your childhood home? The voices that filled your formative years? The spoken and unspoken rules that governed your family?

Your upbringing encompasses everything that shaped you during your most impressionable years—your environment, relationships, the beliefs and values that surrounded you, and most significantly, the messages you received about your worth and potential.

Was your upbringing filled with trauma and chaos, or was it characterized by peace and stability? Were you surrounded by hostility, criticism, and anger? Or did love, patience, and encouragement pave your path? Are you still carrying fears and insecurities from your youth? Do painful memories from abuse or rejection still surface when you close your eyes at night?

THE ABSENCE OF LOVE AND ACCEPTANCE

In many cultures and families, the absence of expressed love isn't necessarily malicious. Many parents demonstrate commitment and loyalty through provision and protection, believing their actions speak louder than words. I witnessed this in my own upbringing—my parents worked tirelessly to give us advantages in life. They provided for our needs, encouraged our education, and supported our interests.

But what was missing—what they had never received from their own parents—was verbal affirmation of our worth. We needed to hear that we were enough, that we were valued for who we were, not just what we accomplished.

Sometimes, in attempts to improve those around us, families resort to comparison, criticism, and conditional approval. Again, often not out of malice, but because that's what was modeled for them.

My parents, though well-intentioned, often compared me to my siblings. When I achieved something, my father's response was frequently, "Couldn't you do better?" This left me feeling like nothing I did was ever good enough. I remember crying myself to sleep, desperately longing for the love and acceptance that seemed just out of reach.

This pattern of tearing down rather than building up is unfortunately common in many communities. To shift our culture, we must start by examining our own mindsets about the power of words and the values we prioritize.

People who grow up feeling like nothing they do is acceptable often develop a belief that they can't do anything right and should expect to fail. This creates a pattern of starting projects but never finishing them, or being so paralyzed by fear of failure that they never begin at all.

The deeper wounds include feeling unlovable, unworthy, and burdensome to others. The results can be emotional insecurity, poor self-image, and an inability to perform to one's potential.

THE IMPACT OF WORDS & FAMILY CULTURE

But how do we combat this? How do we stop the cycle and end the power that our upbringing has over our present choices?

Conversely, those with upbringings full of love, affirmation, and encouragement can sometimes feel insecure about their ability to do the same for others. The high standards set by loving parents can create pressure to live up to seemingly impossible expectations.

Both types of upbringing, when not met with clarity and understanding of our power to choose differently, can stunt our growth and prevent us from stepping into our God-given potential.

TURNING PAIN INTO PURPOSE

For me, prayer, a loving faith community, and staying grounded in God's Word have created strong self-efficacy and belief that no longer uses my upbringing as either a crutch or a hurdle to pursuing my destiny. Instead, these experiences have given me a unique perspective and ability to relate to others while sharing God's message of healing and restoration.

Each time I step on a stage, record a podcast, meet with a client, or teach a class, I'm undoing decades of mental imprisonment and emotional immaturity. I'm proving to that little girl who cried herself to sleep that her worth isn't determined by her performance or others' approval.

Looking back at my career journey reveals God's hand in ways I couldn't have imagined: Cashier, Stock Girl, Shampoo Girl, Tutor, Librarian, Teacher's Assistant, Respite Worker, Trainer, Program Manager, Coordinator, MC, Dean, Program Facilitator, Lead Teacher, Counselor, Coach, CEO, Entrepreneur, Bible Study Leader, Podcast Host.

All aspects of your history contribute to the story that makes you uniquely you. Despite how insignificant or shameful some experiences may seem, they can be used by God to create something so beautiful that it can only bring glory to Him.

KEY TAKEAWAYS:

- ☑ Your internal narrative shapes your reality
- ☑ Upbringing influences but doesn't have to determine your future
- ☑ Generational cycles can be broken with intentional choice
- ☑ God can redeem every part of your story for His purposes
- ☑ Your experiences prepare you for your unique calling

REFLECTION QUESTIONS

1. **Your Personal Narrative:** Write down the story you currently tell yourself about who you are. Be honest—include both positive and negative elements. What patterns do you notice?
2. **Upbringing Assessment:** Describe your childhood environment in detail. What messages did you receive about your worth, potential, and place in the world? Which messages still influence you today?
3. **Identifying Wounds:** What specific experiences or relationships from your past still trigger emotional reactions? Are there people you need to forgive—including yourself?
4. **Recognizing Patterns:** How do these past experiences show up in your current relationships, career choices, and decision-making? Do they make you more empathetic or more guarded?

5. **Generational Cycles:** What patterns from your family of origin do you see yourself repeating? What cycles do you want to break for the next generation?
6. **Redemption Vision:** Looking at your past experiences (including the difficult ones), how might God want to use them to help others? What unique perspective do your struggles give you?
7. **Career Reflection:** List the various roles and jobs you've held. How has each experience prepared you for your current calling or future purpose?

CHAPTER 2:

*"But God chose the foolish things of the world to shame the wise;
God chose the weak things of the world to shame the strong."*
— 1 CORINTHIANS 1:27

Throughout history, God has delighted in choosing the most unlikely candidates to fulfill His purposes. These women didn't become powerful in spite of their difficult backgrounds—they became powerful because God transformed their pain into purpose and their trials into testimonies.

RAHAB: FAITH IN UNLIKELY PLACES

Rahab was a prostitute living in Jericho during one of the most significant military campaigns in biblical history. When Israelite spies came to scout the land, she made a choice that would change everything—she chose to trust in a God she barely knew over the familiar systems that had sustained her.

HER CHOICE

According to an article by Crossroads Church titled "How a Hooker and Her Lies Pleased God," Rahab's story demonstrates that God rewards faith even when it comes in a messy package. God was more interested in her belief and willingness to risk everything for Him than He was in her perfect behavior.

James 2:25-26 mentions Rahab as being considered righteous for what she did when she gave lodging to the spies and sent them off in a different direction. Her lies to protect God's people were actually acts of faith.

HER LEGACY

Matthew 1:5 reveals that Rahab became part of Jesus' genealogy—this former prostitute became an ancestor of the Messiah. Her story challenges our understanding of whom God chooses and why.

LESSONS FROM RAHAB'S LIFE:

1. **Recognize God as God:** She didn't know Him well, but she truly believed what she knew. Faith doesn't require perfect theology; it requires genuine trust.
2. **Risk something for Him:** Rahab risked her city and her life on this God she barely knew. She threw in all her chips with God.
3. **Act on your beliefs:** It wasn't enough for Rahab to believe; when the opportunity came to put her faith into action, she didn't hesitate.

Like Rahab, many women today feel disqualified by their past choices or current circumstances. But God doesn't look at our resume—He looks at our heart and our willingness to trust Him with our future.

RUTH: LOYALTY & NEW BEGINNINGS

Ruth was a Moabite woman who married an Israelite and, after his death, chose to remain with her mother-in-law Naomi rather than return to her own people. This decision defied logic from every practical standpoint—financial, cultural, and social.

Ruth's famous declaration—"Where you go I will go, and where you stay I will stay. Your people will be my people and your God my God" (Ruth 1:16)—wasn't just about loyalty to Naomi. It was about choosing to follow the God of Abraham, Isaac, and Jacob.

After experiencing Israelite traditions and customs, Ruth had become a convert in heart. Her love for God and obedience to His leading propelled her forward, ultimately leading to her inclusion in Jesus' genealogy (Matthew 1:5).

Ruth's story shows us that God's family isn't limited by ethnicity, background, or circumstances. Her faithfulness to God's calling led to her becoming the great-grandmother of King David.

MODERN CONNECTION

Ruth represents every woman who has had to leave familiar territory to follow God's calling. Her story encourages us that God honors faithfulness even when it requires significant sacrifice.

MARY MAGDALENE: FROM BROKENNESS TO BOLDNESS

HER STORY

There has been significant controversy over Mary Magdalene's role in the early church, with some attempting to minimize her importance. What we know for certain is that Jesus healed her from seven evil spirits (Luke 8:1-3), and she became one of His most devoted followers.

HER CHOICE

Shortly after being healed, Mary began following Jesus and supporting His ministry along with other women. She wasn't content to simply receive healing—she dedicated her life to serving the One who had set her free.

HER LEGACY

Mary played a prominent role in Jesus' death and resurrection. She was among the last people at the crucifixion, helped prepare His body for burial, and was one of the first witnesses to His resurrection (John 20:1-13).

Mary Magdalene represents every woman who has experienced spiritual, emotional, or psychological bondage. Her story demonstrates that our past doesn't disqualify us from significant ministry—it often prepares us for it.

MARTHA DANDRIDGE: A LEGACY OF SERVICE

Martha Dandridge was born in 1731 as the first of eight children. Unlike most women of her time in Virginia, she learned to read and write early, developing skills that would later serve her nation.

Martha married Daniel Park Custis at 18, becoming a widow seven years later with substantial wealth and property. She remarried George Washington at 27, inheriting not just love but the immense responsibility of being America's first First Lady.

During the Revolutionary War, Martha joined George at winter encampments, caring for soldiers and maintaining crucial communications. Her letters home provided valuable historical records of the war. As First Lady, she set standards for grace, poise, and philanthropy that influenced generations.

After George's death, Martha freed over 120 enslaved people, demonstrating moral leadership even in her grief.

MODERN CONNECTION

Martha Washington shows us that leadership often means serving others, especially during their most difficult moments. Her story encourages women to use their education, resources, and influence for the greater good.

MADAM C.J. WALKER: TURNING TRIALS INTO TRIUMPH

HER STORY

Born Sarah Breedlove in 1867, she was the first child in her family born free after the Emancipation Proclamation. Orphaned at seven, married at fourteen, and widowed at twenty, Sarah faced seemingly insurmountable challenges.

HER CHOICE

After developing a scalp condition that caused hair loss, Sarah created what became known as the "Walker system"—a method involving scalp preparation, lotions, and specialized combs. Rather than simply solving her own problem, she recognized a business opportunity to serve other Black women.

HER LEGACY

Sarah became the first self-made Black female millionaire in America. She built a business empire by employing thousands of women as "beauty culturalists," creating economic opportunities in communities that desperately needed them.

Madam C.J. Walker's story demonstrates how personal struggles can become the foundation for serving others and building something greater than ourselves.

MODERN REFLECTION: WHO ARE THE "UNLIKELY CANDIDATES" TODAY?

These women's stories aren't unique. Every day, women around us are transforming their pain into purpose and their struggles into strength:

- The single mother who creates a nonprofit to help other women escape domestic violence
- The recovering addict who becomes a counselor helping others find sobriety
- The cancer survivor who starts a support group for other patients
- The business owner who hires women transitioning out of prison

God is still choosing unlikely candidates. He's still using broken backgrounds to create beautiful testimonies. The question isn't whether you're qualified—it's whether you're willing.

KEY TAKEAWAYS

- ☑ God chooses unlikely candidates to demonstrate His power
- ☑ Past pain can become present purpose when surrendered to God

- ☑ Faith doesn't require perfect circumstances—it requires genuine trust
- ☑ Your willingness matters more than your credentials
- ☑ Every story of redemption becomes hope for someone else

REFLECTION QUESTIONS

1. **Rahab's Faith:** In what ways does Rahab's story challenge your understanding of God's grace and mercy? How does her inclusion in Jesus' genealogy encourage you about your own past?
2. **Taking Risks:** What has God been asking you to risk for Him? What fears or practical concerns are holding you back from taking that step of faith?
3. **Ruth's Loyalty:** How does Ruth's story demonstrate the power of choosing God's way over cultural expectations? Where in your life do you need Ruth's kind of courage?
4. **Mary's Service:** How can you emulate Mary Magdalene's example of turning from brokenness to devoted service? What healing has God provided that you could use to help others?
5. **Martha's Leadership:** How does Martha Washington's life challenge your understanding of what it means to be a woman of faith and influence? Where is God calling you to serve during difficult times?
6. **Sarah's Innovation:** Like Madam C.J. Walker, how could your personal struggles become the foundation for serving others? What problems have you overcome that others are still facing?
7. **Modern Examples:** Who are the "unlikely candidates" in your community who are making a difference? How does their example inspire you?

8. **Your Qualification:** In what ways do you feel unqualified for God's calling? How do these women's stories speak to those insecurities?
9. **Legacy Building:** What kind of legacy do you want to leave? How can you start building it today, regardless of your background or current circumstances?

OWNING YOUR PRESENT

CHAPTER 3:
THE LORD DETERMINES HER PATH

"In their hearts humans plan their course, but the Lord establishes their steps."
—Proverbs 16:9

DREAMS DEFERRED: LEARNING FROM SETBACKS

Two years ago, God placed an idea on my heart that excited me: creating "A Basket of Comedy for Mommy"—a Mother's Day event combining encouragement, relaxation, and laughter. I believed comedy could be therapy for overwhelmed mothers, and I wanted to package it in a way that would truly bless them.

But I kept getting stuck on the details. Should I use a basket, a box, or a bag? The uncertainty paralyzed me, and I did nothing. Then COVID hit, putting everything on hold. The following year brought our business's first anniversary celebration and commitments to help another small business, so once again, the dream was shelved.

THE POWER OF DETERMINATION

This year, I decided: no more excuses. I purchased everything in advance, spent weekends preparing, and had my husband create DVDs. I found a Mother's Day vendor opportunity—perfect! Someone else would handle the event planning; I'd just show up and do what I do.

The event host gave me prime placement and a microphone. I had my backdrop, branding materials, and promotional shirt. Everything looked perfect from the outside.

WHEN PREPARATION MEETS PURPOSE

Here's what I didn't do: I didn't pray much about the deeper purpose of my presence there. I focused entirely on having the right merchandise and products ready. I treated it like a business transaction rather than a ministry opportunity.

> *"Therefore, since we have a great high priest who has ascended into heaven, Jesus the Son of God, let us hold firmly to the faith we profess."*
>
> —HEBREWS 4:14-16

The five-hour event taught me a humbling lesson. Despite being front and center where everyone could see me, I sold maybe three DVDs—and those were purchased by other vendors who felt sorry for me. After spending over a thousand dollars on the booth, products, website development, and marketing materials, I made thirty dollars.

THE REAL PROBLEM

I had done everything right from a business perspective but failed to prepare mentally and spiritually. I hadn't approached this opportunity as a vessel sent by God to fulfill my purpose. Instead, I treated it like a commercial venture.

MENTAL & SPIRITUAL PREPARATION

Why wasn't I mentally prepared?

I had experienced some negative interactions during the week leading up to the event that put me in a "blah" mindset. Instead of working through those issues or seeking God in sincere prayer, I did superficial devotionals and scripture reading without truly giving my concerns to God.

> *"During the days of Jesus' life on earth, he offered prayers and petitions with fervent cries and tears to the one who could save him from death, and he was heard because of his reverent submission."*
>
> —HEBREWS 5:7

THE HABITS THAT GOT ME HERE

I had gotten away from the practices that built my confidence to show up authentically each week:

- Waking up early for quiet time with God
- Sitting in silence to hear His voice
- Maintaining sacred morning routines
- Protecting my relationship with God as my top priority

Instead, my mornings had become rushed, loud, and distracting. I wasn't making time sacred like I knew I needed to.

WALKING IN ALIGNMENT, NOT JUST AMBITION

THE IMPORTANCE OF PURPOSE CLARITY

I'm clear on why I'm here on earth and what my gifts are. It took time to figure them out, but I know my calling has nothing to do with selling DVDs or t-shirts. When I started functioning outside my purpose, God didn't bless it.

My calling is to encourage and instruct God's people for acts of service. Everything else is secondary.

THE ROLE OF MENTAL STATE

I struggle with seasons of depression, lack of motivation, and unproductive mindsets. I don't want people to think I have it all together—quite the contrary. I'm a work in progress, and the only good I do comes through God and the Holy Spirit.

Sometimes I teeter between healthy confidence and overcompensation for things beyond my control. These negative experiences attacked me mentally because I didn't have my guard up.

LESSONS FROM MY VENDOR STORY

WHAT THIS EXPERIENCE TAUGHT ME:

- **Business success without spiritual alignment is hollow:** All the right logistics mean nothing if you're not walking in purpose.

- **Preparation must be holistic:** Physical, mental, and spiritual preparation are all necessary for meaningful success.
- **Our mindset affects our ministry:** When we're not right internally, it affects our ability to serve others effectively.
- **God honors authentic purpose over profit motives:** When our primary goal is serving rather than selling, God shows up differently.
- **Setbacks can redirect us to our true calling:** Sometimes failure is God's way of getting our attention back on what really matters.

MOVING FORWARD WITH WISDOM

"We have much to say about this, but it is hard to clarify it because you no longer try to understand. Though you ought to be teachers by this time, you need someone to teach you the elementary truths of God's word all over again."

—HEBREWS 5:11-14

This passage convicts me. I had moved away from the foundational practices that kept me spiritually sharp and emotionally stable. I was trying to operate on yesterday's spiritual filling while facing today's challenges.

KEY TAKEAWAYS

- ☑ Dreams delayed aren't necessarily dreams denied
- ☑ Spiritual preparation is as important as practical preparation
- ☑ Purpose must drive profit, not the other way around
- ☑ Mental and emotional health affect our ability to serve effectively
- ☑ Setbacks can be setups for greater clarity and alignment

REFLECTION QUESTIONS

1. **Dreams and Timing:** What idea or dream has God put on your heart that you haven't pursued yet? What has held you back—fear, uncertainty, or other priorities?
2. **Preparation Assessment:** Think about a recent opportunity or challenge. How did you prepare practically versus spiritually? What was the result?
3. **Purpose Clarity:** Do you know your God-given purpose? If so, how well are your current activities aligned with it? If not, what steps can you take to discover it?
4. **Mental State Management:** How do negative interactions or difficult circumstances affect your mindset? What strategies do you have for working through these challenges?
5. **Spiritual Practices:** What habits or practices help you stay connected to God and mentally sharp? Which ones have you gotten away from that you need to restore?
6. **Learning from Setbacks:** Describe a recent disappointment or failure. What lessons did God want to teach you through that experience?
7. **Sacred Time:** How do you protect your relationship with God as your top priority? What changes do you need to make to your daily routine?
8. **Ministry vs. Business:** In what ways might you be treating your calling like a business transaction rather than a ministry opportunity? How can you shift your perspective?

CHAPTER 4:
THE EFFECTS OF FAITH ON HERSTORY

"So too, faith, if it does not have works [to back it up], is by itself dead [inoperative and ineffective]."
—James 2:17 (AMP)

Faith without action is powerless. But faith combined with intentional works becomes a transformative force that not only changes our own lives but creates ripples of impact that touch entire communities.

FAITH + WORKS: WHY BOTH MATTER

From the women we've studied—both biblical and historical—we learn that true faith always produces corresponding action. These women didn't allow their histories to become stumbling blocks; instead, they transformed their past experiences into launching pads for serving others.

> "God is not unjust; he will not forget your work and the love you have shown him as you have helped his people and continue to help them."
>
> —HEBREWS 6:10-12

The difference between women who remain stuck in their past and those who use it for good lies in their response to their experiences. Faith activates our ability to see purpose in our pain and transforms our wounds into wisdom that can heal others.

MODERN WOMEN OF FAITH — LIVING TESTIMONIES

AISHA OLIVER - ROOT2FRUIT CHICAGO

When I think of women who pour into young people, Aisha Oliver immediately comes to mind. As founder and CEO of Root2Fruit in Chicago, Aisha doesn't use her challenging upbringing in her neighborhood as an excuse—she uses it as her "why."

Her personal experiences fuel her determination to:

- Appear on radio stations advocating for her organization
- Write books sharing her story and mission
- Organize pop-up community events feeding the homeless
- Engage young people in revitalizing their own neighborhoods

Aisha's faith turned her painful history into passionate service. She understood that her struggles qualified her to help others facing similar challenges.

Kristina is a model, gospel recording artist, Stellar award winner, and co-host of the 2022 Stellar Awards. Despite these impressive accolades, she finds her deepest purpose through Faith On A Thousand, where her mission is to pour into the lives of a thousand women annually.

Through her organization, Kristina provides:

- Community givebacks
- Mindset workshops
- Interview skills training
- Mental health retreats

Her upbringing, full of love and encouragement, created a desire to ensure other young women have access to the same support system that helped shape her.

My friend Ebony started Brown Bag Charity at the beginning of COVID to collect, provide, and distribute resources to families in need. Much of what she donates comes from her own pocket, demonstrating faith through sacrificial giving.

Ebony organizes:

- Food drives and coat drives
- Back-to-school supply distributions
- Trunk-or-treat parties for families who don't celebrate Halloween
- "Dreams and Visions" vision board parties for mothers

Her personal experiences as a mother and her deeper relationship with God transformed life's challenges into rocket fuel for serving others.

TURNING PAIN INTO SERVICE

WHY THESE STORIES MATTER

These women understand a crucial truth: kindred spirits gravitate toward one another. When you begin using your pain for purpose, you naturally connect with others doing the same work.

I guarantee there are women around you doing similar work who could use encouragement, motivation, or support. The missing ingredient to their ministry might be your specific gift, experience, or perspective.

> *"And let us consider how we may spur one another on toward love and good deeds, not giving up meeting together, as some are in the habit of doing, but encouraging one another."*
> —HEBREWS 10:24-25

THE RIPPLE EFFECT

When we transform our pain into service:

1. **We find healing in helping others** — There's something profoundly healing about using our wounds to help others heal
2. **We create community** — Our service connects us with like-minded people who share our passion
3. **We multiply impact** — Our story gives others permission to transform their own pain into purpose
4. **We honor God** — Our service becomes worship when motivated by gratitude for His redemption in our lives

FINDING YOUR "WHY"

The difference between women who remain victims of their circumstances and those who become victors isn't the absence of pain—it's what they choose to do with their pain.

Ask yourself these questions:

- What experiences in your past caused you the most pain?
- How have those experiences given you unique insight or empathy?
- What would you want to tell someone currently facing what you've overcome?
- How could your story become hope for someone else?

Your past experiences have created values within you. These values drive your actions and decisions. When we don't examine these values consciously, we may find ourselves living inconsistently or feeling constantly conflicted.

As a meditative reflection, consider:

- What values have your past experiences created in you?
- Which of these values serve you well?
- Which values need to be surrendered or transformed?
- How can you ensure your actions align with God-honoring values?

FROM PERSONAL TO PURPOSEFUL

The journey from pain to purpose requires:

1. **Acknowledgment** — Honestly facing what happened to you
2. **Processing** — Working through the emotions and impact with God and trusted others
3. **Perspective** — Asking God to show you His purpose in allowing these experiences
4. **Action** — Taking steps to use your experience to help others
5. **Community** — Connecting with others who share your heart for service

KEY TAKEAWAYS

- ☑ Faith without works is incomplete and ineffective
- ☑ Our pain can become our greatest ministry when surrendered to God
- ☑ Modern women of faith are transforming their communities through service
- ☑ Finding your "why" requires examining your experiences for God's purposes
- ☑ Community amplifies individual impact

REFLECTION QUESTIONS

1. **Faith and Works:** How have your personal history and experiences affected your current actions and beliefs? Where do you see your faith producing corresponding works?

2. **Overcoming Obstacles:** Have you ever allowed your past to become a stumbling block in moving forward? How did you (or how could you) overcome it?
3. **Pain into Purpose:** How can you use your personal experiences as a catalyst for doing good in the lives of others? What unique perspective do your struggles provide?
4. **Modern Inspiration:** Have you ever been inspired by someone like Aisha Oliver, Kristina Holloway, or Ebony Guerrier to take action? What stopped you or motivated you to act?
5. **Community Involvement:** How can you use your gifts to encourage and motivate others who may be doing similar work in your community?
6. **Values Assessment:** What values have your past experiences created in you? Which ones serve God's purposes, and which ones need to be transformed?
7. **Consistency Check:** How can you ensure that your actions and beliefs are consistent with God-honoring values?
8. **Service Opportunities:** What problems in your community could you help solve based on your unique experiences and gifts?
9. **Legacy Vision:** How can faith play a role in shifting your past experiences for good and motivating you to take action toward positive change?

RENEWING YOUR MIND

CHAPTER 5:
HER THOUGHTS DETERMINE HER STORY

> *"Do not conform to the pattern of this world, but be transformed by the renewing of your mind. Then you will be able to test and approve what God's will is—his good, pleasing and perfect will."*
> —Romans 12:2

Your thoughts are the architects of your reality. The mental patterns you've developed over years of experience create the lens through which you see yourself, others, and your possibilities. But here's the powerful truth: you have the ability to change those patterns.

THE POWER OF THOUGHT PATTERNS

Imagine someone describing you to a friend before you all meet. How would they capture who you are? Now, more importantly, how do you describe yourself to yourself? What internal narrative runs through your mind about your worth, capabilities, and future?

This internal dialogue shapes everything—how you handle stress, interact with others, pursue opportunities, and respond to setbacks. But where did these thought patterns originate?

THE FORMATION OF MENTAL PATTERNS

Our thought patterns develop through:

- **Family Messages:** What we heard about ourselves growing up
- **Cultural Influences:** The values and beliefs of our communities
- **Personal Experiences:** How we interpreted events that happened to us
- **Spiritual Formation:** What we believe about God and our relationship with Him

These influences create mental highways—well-traveled paths of thinking that become our default responses to life.

IDENTIFYING LIMITING BELIEFS

COMMON LIMITING BELIEFS FOR WOMEN:

"I'm not good enough."
This belief often stems from comparison, criticism, or conditional love in childhood. It shows up as perfectionism, people-pleasing, or avoiding challenges.

"People can't be trusted."
Born from betrayal or disappointment, this belief creates walls that prevent authentic relationships and opportunities.

"I don't matter."
When our voices weren't heard or our needs weren't met, we may believe our opinions, dreams, and presence aren't valuable.

"I have to do everything myself."
This develops when others consistently let us down, leading to difficulty delegating, accepting help, or building teams.

"I don't deserve good things."
Rooted in shame or unworthiness, this belief causes us to sabotage success or settle for less than God's best.

HOW THESE BELIEFS AFFECT OUR LIVES

If we believe people can't be trusted, we show up guarded and suspicious. If we believe we're not good enough, we play small and minimize our impact. If we believe we don't matter, we hide our gifts because we don't think people will understand or appreciate them.

These beliefs aren't acts of faith—they're acts of fear that limit our ability to serve God and others effectively.

PRACTICING A NEW IDENTITY IN CHRIST

As Christians, we're called to leave our old ways of thinking behind and embrace a new identity. Romans 6:4 explains that just as Christ was raised from the dead, we too may live a new life.

The Amplified Bible explains: "In the Church of Paul's day, full submersion was the usual form of baptism—new Christians were buried entirely in water. They understood this to symbolize the death and burial of the old way of life. Coming up out of the water symbolized resurrection to new life with Christ."

THE DAILY CHOICE

This transformation isn't a one-time event—it's a daily choice. Twenty years into my Christian journey, I'm still learning that the "newness of life" the Bible talks about requires daily decisions to walk in God's ways rather than lean on my own understanding.

TAKING ON NEW ROLES

Think about the different roles you've embraced in womanhood—sister, daughter, mother, wife, professional. None of these roles came with automatic knowledge. You learned how to function in each one through daily practice.

The same is true with your identity in Christ. You must put on this new identity each day and practice walking in it.

DAILY MENTAL RENEWAL PRACTICES

1. MORNING SCRIPTURE MEDITATION

Start each day by reading Scripture that affirms your identity in Christ:

- "I am fearfully and wonderfully made" (Psalm 139:14)
- "I can do all things through Christ who strengthens me" (Philippians 4:13)
- "God has plans to prosper me and not to harm me" (Jeremiah 29:11)

Throughout the day, pay attention to your internal dialogue. When negative thoughts arise:

- Acknowledge them without judgment
- Ask: "Is this thought true? Is it helpful? Does it align with God's Word?"
- Replace lies with truth

When limiting beliefs surface, take them to God in prayer: "Father, I recognize this thought pattern that's been holding me back. I surrender this lie to You and ask You to renew my mind with Your truth."

Regularly declare who you are in Christ:

- "I am chosen and beloved by God"
- "I am equipped for every good work"
- "I am more than a conqueror through Christ"

5. COMMUNITY ACCOUNTABILITY

Surround yourself with people who will speak truth into your life and challenge limiting beliefs when they see them operating.

HELPING OTHERS DO THE SAME

THE RIPPLE EFFECT OF RENEWED THINKING

As you experience the freedom that comes from renewed thinking, you naturally become a source of encouragement for others. Your transformation gives others permission to examine their own thought patterns.

PRACTICAL WAYS TO HELP OTHERS:

1. **Share your story** — Be vulnerable about your own journey of mental renewal
2. **Ask good questions** — Help others identify their limiting beliefs
3. **Speak truth** — Lovingly challenge lies others believe about themselves
4. **Model healthy thinking** — Show what renewed thinking looks like in action
5. **Provide resources** — Share books, scriptures, or tools that helped you

BREAKING GENERATIONAL PATTERNS

One of the most powerful ways to help others is to break generational patterns of thinking in your own family. When you choose to think differently, you give your children, siblings, and extended family a new model to follow.

KEY TAKEAWAYS

- ☑ Your thoughts create your reality
- ☑ Limiting beliefs can be identified and replaced
- ☑ Mental renewal is a daily practice, not a one-time event
- ☑ Your identity in Christ must be practiced intentionally
- ☑ Helping others renew their minds multiplies your impact

REFLECTION QUESTIONS

1. **Thought Patterns:** What are some old thought patterns you struggle with? How do they affect your daily life, relationships, and decision-making?
2. **Christian Identity:** How has your understanding of being a new creation in Christ evolved over time? What aspects of this identity do you find most challenging to embrace?
3. **Role Assessment:** What role do your responsibilities and duties as a woman play in your self-identity? Which roles energize you and which ones drain you?
4. **Limiting Beliefs:** What limiting beliefs do you recognize in your thinking? Where did these beliefs originate, and how do they currently affect your choices?
5. **Renewal Practices:** What steps can you take to consciously treat the desires and temptations of your old nature as dead? What daily practices help you renew your mind?
6. **Thought Impact:** How do your thought patterns shape the way you interact with the world and those around you? What would change if you thought differently?

7. **Transformation Steps:** What specific steps can you take to overcome old patterns of thought and live more fully in your new identity in Christ?
8. **Faith vs. Fear:** How can you cultivate a mindset of faith instead of one rooted in fear and mistrust? What would bold faith look like in your daily life?
9. **Helping Others:** How can you encourage others who may not have yet found their identity in Christ? What would it look like to help others renew their minds?

EMBRACING YOUR LIFETIME ASSIGNMENT

CHAPTER 6:
REASONS, SEASONS, AND A LIFETIME

"For I know the plans I have for you," declares the Lord, "plans to prosper you and not to harm you, to give you hope and a future."
—JEREMIAH 29:11

You trust the bus driver you've never met. You relax on planes piloted by strangers. So why do you worry when you know who's driving your destiny?

WHO'S DRIVING YOUR DESTINY?

Whatever happens in your life—whether you understand it, whether you feel like you deserve it—there is a reason for everything. In the end, you will understand the purpose because it will take you exactly where you're supposed to be. It may not be where you wanted to be or where you thought you'd be, but it's exactly where God needs you to be.

THE COMPARISON TRAP

We tell our girlfriends everything without them asking, but struggle to pray consistently to the Lord of the universe. We scroll social media for hours and read countless posts, but have little idea what God's Word says about who we are.

We're quick to compare ourselves to other women—their accomplishments, their seeming success, their opportunities—wondering why we can't do what they've done or achieve what they've achieved. But how often do we look at Jesus' influence in His community and His pattern of serving others first, then make excuses about why we can't follow His example?

The irony is that we have access to the same power source that enabled Jesus' ministry.

SOUL, SPIRIT, AND BODY – ALIGNING ALL THREE

UNDERSTANDING OUR THREE PARTS

1 Thessalonians 5:23 mentions spirit, soul, and body—not as separate parts of a person, but as the entire being. This expression emphasizes that God must be involved in every aspect of life. We can't separate spiritual life from everything else or live for God only one day per week.

THE SOUL: YOUR PERSONALITY

The word "soul" and "psychology" come from the same root. Your soul is essentially your personality—your mind, will, and emotions. This is how you relate to other people.

Your body is the house or vehicle through which you communicate with and relate to other humans. People-to-people interaction is guided mainly through your soul.

Your spirit interacts with and connects to God. When you're born physically, you can relate to the world around you. When you're born again through spirit and water into Christ, you gain the capacity to interact with God.

LETTING GO OF COMPARISON

Being born again doesn't erase everything your soul experienced. It means you now have the ability, power, and authority through the Holy Spirit to overcome the hard-wiring of your upbringing and past experiences.

2 Corinthians 5:17 tells us that Christians are brand new people on the inside. The Holy Spirit gives them new life, and they're not the same anymore. We're not reformed, rehabilitated, or re-educated—we're recreated, living in vital union with Christ.

This isn't just individual transformation. A new order of creative energy began with Christ—a new covenant, new perspective, new body, new church. All creation is being renewed.

This requires a new way of looking at all people and all creation. Does your life reflect this new perspective?

THE CHALLENGE OF GRADUAL GROWTH

Christianity isn't a magic pill. Jesus spent three years walking with, training, and loving the twelve men who followed Him. It wasn't until after He was crucified, resurrected, and had left them that they became what He envisioned them being.

The gift of the Holy Spirit was the missing ingredient for them to take action, leaving their old lives of doubt, fear, and stagnation behind.

LIVING FOR LEGACY, NOT JUST TODAY

THE CHOICE BEFORE US

We have the same opportunity today. What will it take for you to pick up your cross and follow Jesus? What old ways, thoughts, and perspectives do you need to leave behind? What ideologies and self-image need to be crucified so you can live a new life that glorifies Christ?

SERVING TWO MASTERS

A person cannot serve two masters; they will either love one and hate the other, or be lukewarm in all their actions. I've ridden the thin line of puffing up my soul to appeal to more people while simultaneously quenching the Spirit's fire.

Ironically, as I take better care of my spirit—finding more ways to connect with God, hearing His voice, feeling His Spirit, and being led by His commands—my soul has never been more attractive to others.

For some people in your life, you may be the only Jesus they see. How are you feeding their spirit? Or are you more concerned with how people receive your soul?

DAILY CHOICES, ETERNAL IMPACT

Who are you leading to Christ today? If you aren't on that list, we need to address that.

Why has it become hard to get out of bed? Why does your soul feel crushed under responsibilities? Why does your heart feel broken?

You're not alone—we all go through these seasons. But to get through them, we must understand what's happening and why. We need to know who we are and understand the stories that have shaped our lives.

Your story has power. It can help you find your way out of depression, anxiety, and mental health struggles. It can help you reach your goals and give you peace of mind. Your story is valuable—it's uniquely yours!

There's no time like the present to start understanding yourself better than ever.

THE ULTIMATE TRUTH

History determines your story, but you determine how it ends. Your past shaped you, but your choices shape your future. God has given you everything you need to write a beautiful ending to your story—one that brings Him glory and blesses others.

KEY TAKEAWAYS

- ☑ God is sovereignly directing your life's journey
- ☑ You are a three-part being that must be aligned with God's purposes
- ☑ Comparison steals joy and distracts from your unique calling
- ☑ Your daily choices create either eternal impact or temporary satisfaction
- ☑ Your story has power to heal both yourself and others

REFLECTION QUESTIONS

1. **Divine Direction:** How does the idea of "God driving your destiny" compare to your daily worries and anxieties? What would change if you truly trusted His guidance?
2. **Interaction Patterns:** How do you typically interact with God compared to how you interact with your friends? What does this reveal about your priorities?
3. **Comparison Habits:** How often do you compare yourself to others? How has this comparison affected your life and your sense of calling?

4. **Soul Expression:** How does your soul (personality, mind, will, emotions) play a role in your interactions with others? Is it aligned with your spirit?
5. **Spiritual Rebirth:** How does being born again through spirit and water affect the hard-wiring of your upbringing? What changes have you noticed?
6. **New Creation:** Do you believe that Christians are truly brand new people on the inside? What evidence of this transformation do you see in your own life?
7. **New Perspective:** What is the new perspective that comes with being a Christian? How does it change the way you see all people and all creation?
8. **Holy Spirit's Role:** How does the gift of the Holy Spirit help you take action and follow Jesus? Where do you need His power in your life?
9. **Cross-Carrying:** What do you need to leave behind in order to follow Jesus more fully? What old ways of thinking or living need to die?
10. **Daily Impact:** How can you make sure that your daily choices are drawing you closer to Jesus and creating eternal impact rather than temporary satisfaction?

LIVING IT OUT

CHAPTER 7:
FROM HERSTORY TO LEGACY

> *"She is clothed with strength and dignity; she can laugh at the days to come. She speaks with wisdom, and faithful instruction is on her tongue."*
> —PROVERBS 31:25-26

Your story was never meant to end with you. Every experience you've had, every lesson you've learned, every breakthrough you've experienced—it's all been preparation for something greater. You're not just healing for yourself; you're healing to help heal others.

FINDING MEANING IN YOUR STORY

While personal healing is essential, it's not the final destination. God didn't rescue you just so you could live a comfortable life—He rescued you so you could become a rescuer of others.

Your story becomes meaningful when you:

- Recognize God's faithfulness in bringing you through difficulties
- Identify the lessons He taught you in the process
- Discover how your experience can help others facing similar challenges
- Take action to share your story and serve others

THE REDEMPTION PROCESS

Romans 8:28 promises that "all things work together for good to those who love God, to those who are called according to His purpose." This doesn't mean all things are good—it means God can bring good out of all things when we surrender them to Him.

Your painful experiences become redemptive when they:

1. Draw you closer to God
2. Develop character and compassion in you
3. Prepare you to help others
4. Bring glory to God through your testimony

PRACTICAL WAYS TO SERVE OTHERS

START WHERE YOU ARE

You don't need a formal ministry or perfect life to begin serving others. Start with what you have, where you are.

Ways Experience Can Help Others

If you've overcome addiction:
- Volunteer at recovery centers
- Mentor someone newly sober
- Share your story at meetings
- Support families affected by addiction

If you've survived abuse:
- Volunteer at shelters or crisis centers
- Support legislation protecting victims
- Mentor survivors beginning their healing journey
- Contribute to organizations serving those affected

If you've navigated divorce:
- Lead support groups for divorcing women
- Mentor single mothers
- Provide practical help (childcare, meals, transportation)
- Advocate for resources supporting single-parent families

If you've overcome financial hardship:
- Teach financial literacy classes
- Mentor women starting businesses
- Support job training programs
- Share practical money management skills

If you've battled depression or anxiety:
- Advocate for mental health awareness
- Support others seeking help
- Share resources and coping strategies
- Normalize conversations about mental health

PROFESSIONAL INTEGRATION

Consider how your career can become a platform for ministry:

- Teachers can mentor struggling students
- Healthcare workers can provide extra compassion and prayer
- Business owners can create opportunities for others
- Artists can use creativity to inspire and heal
- Leaders can develop other women's potential

BUILDING COMMUNITY & SISTERHOOD

THE POWER OF CONNECTION

Healing happens in community. When women share their stories authentically, it creates space for others to do the same.

CREATING SAFE SPACES

Whether formal or informal, create environments where women can:

- Share their stories without judgment
- Receive prayer and encouragement
- Learn from each other's experiences
- Build genuine friendships
- Support each other's growth

WAYS TO BUILD COMMUNITY:

1. Start a small group focused on healing, growth, or Bible study
2. Organize regular gatherings for fellowship and encouragement
3. Create online communities for women facing similar challenges

4. Host events that combine fun with meaningful connection
5. Facilitate workshops teaching practical life skills
6. Establish mentoring relationships between women of different life stages

Every woman needs mentors—and every woman can be a mentor. You don't need to have all the answers; you just need to be a few steps ahead in some area of life.

Effective mentoring includes:

- Listening more than speaking
- Asking good questions that promote reflection
- Sharing your story authentically
- Providing practical guidance and resources
- Praying for and with your mentee
- Connecting them with other helpful people

PASSING DOWN A FAITHFUL LEGACY

Your healing affects not just you, but generations after you. When you break cycles of pain, dysfunction, or limiting beliefs, you give your children and their children a different model to follow.

Think about what you want to be remembered for:

- What values do you want to pass down?

- What lessons do you want your children to learn from your life?
- How do you want to impact your community?
- What would you want written about your life?

LEGACY IN ACTION

Your legacy isn't something that happens after you die—it's being built every day through:

- The values you model
- The love you show
- The service you provide
- The courage you demonstrate
- The faith you live

INVESTING IN THE NEXT GENERATION

Make intentional investments in younger women:

- Sponsor someone's education or training
- Create opportunities for someone to develop their gifts
- Introduce others to people who can help them
- Share your platform to amplify someone else's voice
- Invest financially in causes serving women and girls

DOCUMENTATION AND STORYTELLING

Don't let your story die with you:

- Write your story for your family
- Record videos sharing life lessons
- Create photo albums with meaningful captions

- Write letters to be opened at important milestones
- Share your testimony publicly when appropriate

Your legacy isn't something that starts when you die—it's what you're building right now. Every conversation, every act of service, every choice to love instead of judge, every decision to forgive instead of hold grudges—all of this contributes to the legacy you're creating.

KEY TAKEAWAYS

- ☑ Your story becomes meaningful when used to help others
- ☑ Service opportunities exist wherever you are, based on what you've overcome
- ☑ Community and sisterhood are essential for healing and growth
- ☑ Legacy is built daily through your choices and actions
- ☑ Your healing has generational impact beyond what you can see

REFLECTION QUESTIONS

1. **Story Meaning:** How has your understanding of your life story evolved? Where do you now see God's hand in experiences that once only brought pain?
2. **Service Calling:** Based on what you've overcome or learned, what specific ways could you serve others? What holds you back from beginning?
3. **Community Building:** How can you contribute to building community and sisterhood among women? What unique gifts do you bring to relationships?

4. **Mentoring:** Who could you mentor based on your life experience? Who do you need as a mentor in areas where you're still growing?
5. **Generational Impact:** What cycles are you breaking or positive patterns are you establishing for the next generation? How are you being intentional about this?
6. **Legacy Vision:** What do you want to be remembered for? How are your current choices building toward that legacy?
7. **Professional Ministry:** How can your career or skills become a platform for serving others and sharing God's love?
8. **Documentation:** What parts of your story and lessons learned should you document for others? How will you preserve these for future generations?
9. **Next Steps:** What one specific action will you take this week to begin using your story to help someone else?

TOOLS & RESOURCES

WEEK 1: FOUNDATION BUILDING

DAYS 1-7: ESTABLISHING YOUR IDENTITY IN CHRIST

- ☑ **Morning:** Read one verse about your identity in Christ
- ☑ **Afternoon:** Replace one negative thought with God's truth
- ☑ **Evening:** Journal about how you saw God's faithfulness that day

- **Day 1:** Psalm 139:14 — "I am fearfully and wonderfully made"
- **Day 2:** Jeremiah 29:11 — "God has plans to prosper me"
- **Day 3:** Philippians 4:13 — "I can do all things through Christ"
- **Day 4:** 2 Corinthians 5:17 — "I am a new creation"
- **Day 5:** Ephesians 2:10 — "I am God's workmanship"
- **Day 6:** 1 Peter 2:9 — "I am chosen and beloved"
- **Day 7:** Romans 8:37 — "I am more than a conqueror"

WEEK 2: EXAMINING YOUR STORY

DAYS 8-14: UNDERSTANDING YOUR PAST

DAILY PRACTICE:

- ☑ Morning: Pray for clarity about your past
- ☑ Afternoon: Write about one childhood memory and look for God's presence
- ☑ Evening: Thank God for how He's been faithful throughout your life

REFLECTION PROMPTS:

- **Day 8:** What messages about your worth did you receive growing up?
- **Day 9:** What painful experience has taught you the most?
- **Day 10:** How has God shown His faithfulness in your most difficult season?
- **Day 11:** What gifts have emerged from your struggles?
- **Day 12:** Who in your past showed you love, and how can you pass that on?
- **Day 13:** What patterns from your family do you want to change?
- **Day 14:** How has your story prepared you to help others?

WEEK 3: RENEWING YOUR MIND

Days 15-21: Transforming Your Thoughts

- ☑ Morning: Identify one limiting belief you carry
- ☑ Afternoon: Find a Bible verse that contradicts that lie
- ☑ Evening: Speak the truth over yourself before bed

- **Day 15:** Self-worth and value
- **Day 16:** Ability and capability
- **Day 17:** Relationships and trust
- **Day 18:** Future and hope
- **Day 19:** Purpose and calling
- **Day 20:** God's love and acceptance
- **Day 21:** Your impact and influence

WEEK 4: LIVING YOUR PURPOSE
Days 22-30: Taking Action

DAILY PRACTICE:

- ☑ Morning: Ask God how you can serve someone today
- ☑ Afternoon: Take one action to help or encourage another person
- ☑ Evening: Reflect on how serving others affected your own heart

SERVICE CHALLENGES:

- **Day 22:** Send an encouraging text to someone struggling
- **Day 23:** Volunteer your time for a cause you care about
- **Day 24:** Share your testimony with someone who needs hope
- **Day 25:** Mentor or advise someone in an area of your strength
- **Day 26:** Create something that blesses others
- **Day 27:** Advocate for someone who needs a voice
- **Day 28:** Forgive someone you've been holding a grudge against
- **Day 29:** Take a step toward a dream God has placed in your heart
- **Day 30:** Plan how you'll continue using your story to help others

DAILY PRAYER PROMPTS

MORNING PRAYERS

- **Monday** — *New Beginnings* "Father, thank You for the gift of a new day and new mercies. Help me see today through Your eyes and respond to every situation with grace. Show me how You want to use my story today to encourage someone else. Amen."
- **Tuesday** — *Trust and Surrender* "Lord, I surrender my plans to You today. Help me trust Your timing and Your ways, even when I don't understand. Give me peace about my past and confidence about my future. Amen."
- **Wednesday** — *Wisdom and Discernment* "God, grant me wisdom for the decisions I need to make today. Help me discern Your voice above all others. Give me courage to act on what You show me. Amen."
- **Thursday** — *Strength and Perseverance* "Father, when I feel weak today, remind me that Your strength is made perfect in my weakness. Help me persevere through challenges and maintain hope in difficult moments. Amen."

- **Friday** — *Gratitude and Joy* "Lord, help me notice Your blessings today. Fill my heart with gratitude for how far You've brought me. Let Your joy be my strength regardless of my circumstances. Amen."
- **Saturday** — *Rest and Renewal* "God, help me find healthy rest today. Renew my mind, refresh my spirit, and restore my soul. Show me how to care for myself so I can better serve others. Amen."
- **Sunday** — *Worship and Community* "Father, help me worship You not just with my words but with my life. Use me to encourage others in their faith journey. Help me be a blessing to my community. Amen."

EVENING PRAYERS

REFLECTION AND GRATITUDE

"Thank You, God, for Your faithfulness today. Help me see where You were working, even in difficult moments. I surrender any disappointments or frustrations to You. Amen."

FORGIVENESS AND RELEASE

"Father, if I've hurt anyone today, help me make it right. If anyone has hurt me, help me forgive. I release all bitterness and choose to sleep in peace. Amen."

PREPARATION FOR TOMORROW

"Lord, prepare my heart for tomorrow. Give me restful sleep and wake me with excitement for how You'll use me. Help me be ready for whatever You have planned. Amen."

JOURNAL PAGE TEMPLATES

DAILY REFLECTION TEMPLATE

Date: _____

- Scripture of the Day:
- What I'm Grateful For:
- How I Saw God Today:
- One Way I Used My Story to Help Someone:
- One Thing I Learned About Myself:
- Prayer for Tomorrow:

WEEKLY STORY REVIEW TEMPLATE

Week of: _____

Theme This Week: _____

- Biggest Challenge I Faced:
- How God Helped Me Through It:
- What This Experience Taught Me:
- How I Can Use This Learning to Help Others:
- Next Week I Want to Focus On:

MONTHLY LEGACY ASSESSMENT

Month: _____

- How Did I Live My Values This Month?
- What Impact Did I Have on Others?
- What Patterns Am I Seeing in My Growth?
- What Do I Need to Change or Improve?
- How Is God Shaping My Story for His Glory?

ENCOURAGEMENT FOR FINDING MENTORS & COMMUNITY

FINDING A MENTOR

WHAT TO LOOK FOR

- Someone who embodies qualities you want to develop
- A person who has overcome challenges similar to yours
- Someone who points you toward God rather than themselves
- A woman who is honest about her struggles and growth
- Someone who has time and willingness to invest in you

WHERE TO FIND MENTORS

- Your local church or faith community
- Professional or industry organizations
- Community service organizations
- Online faith-based communities
- Through mutual friends or colleagues

HOW TO APPROACH A POTENTIAL MENTOR

- Be specific about what you're looking for
- Respect their time by being prepared for conversations
- Show appreciation for their investment in you
- Be teachable and willing to implement their guidance
- Understand that not everyone can say yes, and that's okay

BUILDING COMMUNITY

CREATING CONNECTION:

- Start small—even 2-3 women can form a meaningful community
- Be vulnerable first to give others permission to open up
- Focus on authentic relationship rather than perfect events
- Make gathering regularly a priority
- Create space for both fun and deep conversation

SUSTAINING COMMUNITY:

- Rotate hosting responsibilities
- Be flexible with scheduling and life changes
- Celebrate each other's victories and support during struggles
- Maintain confidentiality and trust
- Keep God at the center of your relationships

BOOKS FOR CONTINUED GROWTH

- "Uninvited" by Lysa TerKeurst
- "Breaking Free" by Beth Moore
- "The Purpose Driven Life" by Rick Warren
- "Battlefield of the Mind" by Joyce Meyer

- "The Gifts of Imperfection" by Brené Brown
- "Healing the Shame That Binds You" by John Bradshaw
- "Boundaries" by Henry Cloud and John Townsend
- "Get Out of Your Head" by Jennie Allen

LEGACY AND SERVICE:

- "A Purpose Driven Life" by Rick Warren
- "The Circle Maker" by Mark Batterson
- "Anything" by Jennie Allen
- "Live Your Calling" by Kevin and Kay Marie Brennfleck

PODCASTS FOR INSPIRATION

- "Therapy for Black Girls"
- "The Nicole Lapin Podcast"
- "Proverbs 31 Ministries Podcast"
- "The Dave Ramsey Show" (for financial wisdom)
- "Joyce Meyer Enjoying Everyday Life"

ONLINE COMMUNITIES

- She Reads Truth (online Bible study community)
- Proverbs 31 Ministries Online Community
- Local church Facebook groups
- MOPS (Mothers of Preschoolers) groups
- Professional women's organizations in your area

FINAL BLESSING & CALL TO ACTION

A PRAYER FOR YOU, SISTER

Father God,

Thank You for the woman reading these words right now. You know every detail of her story—every joy, every pain, every triumph, and every struggle. You have walked with her through every season, even when she couldn't see You or feel Your presence.

I pray that through this journey of discovering how her history shapes her story, she has gained new eyes to see Your faithfulness, Your purpose, and Your love. Help her understand that nothing in her past was wasted—that You can redeem every experience for Your glory and the good of others.

Give her courage to step boldly into her calling. When fear whispers "you're not qualified," help her remember that You specialize in using unlikely candidates. When shame tries to silence her story, remind her that her testimony has power to set others free.

Surround her with a community of faith-filled women who will encourage her journey and hold her accountable to live in her God-given identity. Bring mentors into her life who will pour wisdom into her, and bring younger women that she can pour into.

Help her see herself as You see her—beloved, chosen, equipped, and sent. May she walk in the confidence that comes from knowing she is Yours and that You have good plans for her life.

Use her story, Father. Use every chapter—the painful ones and the beautiful ones—to help others find their way to You. May her life be a living testament to Your redemptive power and unfailing love.

We love You and trust You with our stories. In Jesus' name, Amen.

YOUR STORY MATTERS—
SHARE IT

Your journey through this book is just the beginning. Now comes the most important part: living out what you've discovered.

Your story has power because:

- It proves God's faithfulness to others going through similar struggles
- It gives hope to women who feel stuck in their past
- It demonstrates that transformation is possible through Christ
- It multiplies the impact of God's work in your life

I want to hear from you:

If this book has impacted your life, please share your story with me. Your testimony could be the encouragement another woman needs to begin her own healing journey.

WAYS TO CONNECT:

- Email me your story: jorioneale@gmail.com
- Share on social media using #HistoryDeterminesHerstory
- Leave a review sharing how this book helped you
- Recommend it to a friend who needs to hear this message

If God has called you to write your own book:

- One of the most powerful ways to use your story is to write it down. If you feel called to share your testimony through writing, I'd love to help you navigate that journey.
- Contact me for a StoryBook Chatl: https://calendly.com/iyhinnertainme/15-minute-chat

Let's discover what's possible when you combine your story with God's power and a clear plan for sharing it with the world.

REMEMBER THIS TRUTH

History determines your story, but you determine how it ends.

Your past shaped you, but it doesn't have to define you. God has given you everything you need to write a beautiful ending—one that brings Him glory and blesses others.

The world is waiting for what only you can offer. Your unique combination of experiences, gifts, and calling is needed in this generation.

Step boldly into your purpose. Share your story. Change the world.

You were made for this.

ACKNOWLEDGMENTS

Thank you for taking this journey with me. Writing and sharing my story is both an honor and a responsibility I don't take lightly.

To every woman who has shared her story with me, trusted me with her pain, and allowed me to witness her transformation—thank you. You have taught me more about God's grace than any book or sermon ever could.

To my husband, Ron O'Neale, your consistent love and support of my calling has made everything possible. Your leadership through service to our family and community provides the stable foundation that allows me to step boldly into ministry. Our sons are blessed to have such an example of godly manhood.

To my children, you inspire me daily to break generational cycles and build something beautiful for you to inherit. May you always know your worth, understand your purpose, and walk confidently in God's calling on your lives.

To the women who blazed trails before us—both the biblical heroes and the modern pioneers—thank you for showing us what's possible when we surrender our stories to God's purposes.

And to you, dear reader—thank you for believing that your story matters. Thank you for doing the hard work of healing. Thank you for choosing to use your pain for purpose. The world is brighter because you're in it.

God bless your journey forward.

ABOUT THE AUTHOR

Jori O'Neale is a speaker, author, podcast host, and encourager who specializes in helping women discover purpose in their pain and transform their stories into powerful testimonies.

Through her speaking, coaching, and writing, Jori has helped thousands of women break free from limiting beliefs, heal from past wounds, and step boldly into their God-given calling.

When not traveling or writing, Jori enjoys time with her husband and children, exploring new coffee shops, and connecting with women who are ready to change the world with their stories.

Connect with Jori:

- **Website:** https://jorioneale.com
- **Podcast:** "Thirty Minutes of Power"
- **Social Media:** @jorioneale
- **Speaking Inquiries:** jorioneale@gmail.com
- **Book Writing Support:** https://calendly.com/iyhinnertainme/15-minute-chat

If you've been inspired by this book, please consider leaving a review and sharing it with a friend who needs to hear this message. Together, we can help more women discover that their history doesn't determine their destiny—God does.

COMPREHENSIVE REFERENCE TABLE

BIBLICAL REFERENCES

SCRIPTURE REFERENCE	TEXT LOCATION IN BOOK	FULL CITATION
Psalm 139:14	Chapter 1, 5, Tools & Resources	"I praise you because I am fearfully and wonderfully made; your works are wonderful, I know that full well." (Psalm 139:14, NIV 1983)
Psalm 139:23-24	Chapter 1 Opening	"Search me, God, and know my heart, test me and know my anxious thoughts. See if there is any offensive way in me, and lead me in the way everlasting." (Psalm 139:23-24, NIV 1983)
Jeremiah 29:11	Chapter 6, Tools & Resources	"'For I know the plans I have for you,' declares the Lord, 'plans to prosper you and not to harm you, to give you hope and a future.'" (Jeremiah 29:11, NIV 1983)
Proverbs 16:9	Chapter 3 Opening	"In their hearts humans plan their course, but the Lord establishes their steps." (Proverbs 16:9, NIV 1983)

SCRIPTURE REFERENCE	TEXT LOCATION IN BOOK	FULL CITATION
Proverbs 31:25-26	Chapter 7 Opening	"She is clothed with strength and dignity; she can laugh at the days to come. She speaks with wisdom, and faithful instruction is on her tongue." (Proverbs 31:25-26, NIV 1983)
Ruth 1:16	Chapter 2	"But Ruth replied, 'Don't urge me to leave you or to turn back from you. Where you go I will go, and where you stay I will stay. Your people will be my people and your God my God.'" (Ruth 1:16, NIV 1983)

NEW TESTAMENT – NIV 1983

SCRIPTURE REFERENCE	TEXT LOCATION IN BOOK	FULL CITATION
Matthew 1:5	Chapter 2	"Salmon the father of Boaz, whose mother was Rahab, Boaz the father of Obed, whose mother was Ruth, Obed the father of Jesse." (Matthew 1:5, NIV 1983)

SCRIPTURE REFERENCE	TEXT LOCATION IN BOOK	FULL CITATION
Luke 8:1-3	Chapter 2	"After this, Jesus traveled about from one town and village to another, proclaiming the good news of the kingdom of God. The Twelve were with him, and also some women who had been cured of evil spirits and diseases: Mary (called Magdalene) from whom seven demons had come out." (Luke 8:1-3, NIV 1983)
John 20:1-13	Chapter 2	"Early on the first day of the week, while it was still dark, Mary Magdalene went to the tomb and saw that the stone had been removed from the entrance... Mary stood outside the tomb crying." (John 20:1-13, NIV 1983)
Romans 6:4	Chapter 5	"We were therefore buried with him through baptism into death in order that, just as Christ was raised from the dead through the glory of the Father, we too may live a new life." (Romans 6:4, NIV 1983)
Romans 8:28	Chapter 7	"And we know that in all things God works for the good of those who love him, who have been called according to his purpose." (Romans 8:28, NIV 1983)

SCRIPTURE REFERENCE	TEXT LOCATION IN BOOK	FULL CITATION
Romans 8:37	Tools & Resources	"No, in all these things we are more than conquerors through him who loved us." (Romans 8:37, NIV 1983)
Romans 12:2	Chapter 5 Opening	"Do not conform to the pattern of this world, but be transformed by the renewing of your mind. Then you will be able to test and approve what God's will is—his good, pleasing and perfect will." (Romans 12:2, NIV 1983)
1 Corinthians 1:27	Chapter 2 Opening	"But God chose the foolish things of the world to shame the wise; God chose the weak things of the world to shame the strong." (1 Corinthians 1:27, NIV 1983)
2 Corinthians 5:17	Chapter 6	"Therefore, if anyone is in Christ, the new creation has come: The old has gone, the new is here!" (2 Corinthians 5:17, NIV 1983)
Ephesians 2:10	Tools & Resources	"For we are God's handiwork, created in Christ Jesus to do good works, which God prepared in advance for us to do." (Ephesians 2:10, NIV 1983)
Philippians 4:13	Chapter 1, Tools & Resources	"I can do all this through him who gives me strength." (Philippians 4:13, NIV 1983)

SCRIPTURE REFERENCE	TEXT LOCATION IN BOOK	FULL CITATION
1 Thessalonians 5:23	Chapter 6	"May God himself, the God of peace, sanctify you through and through. May your whole spirit, soul and body be kept blameless at the coming of our Lord Jesus Christ." (1 Thessalonians 5:23, NIV 1983)
Hebrews 4:14-16	Chapter 3	"Therefore, since we have a great high priest who has ascended into heaven, Jesus the Son of God, let us hold firmly to the faith we profess. For we do not have a high priest who is unable to empathize with our weaknesses, but we have one who has been tempted in every way, just as we are—yet he did not sin. Let us then approach God's throne of grace with confidence, so that we may receive mercy and find grace to help us in our time of need." (Hebrews 4:14-16, NIV 1983)
Hebrews 5:7	Chapter 3	"During the days of Jesus' life on earth, he offered prayers and petitions with fervent cries and tears to the one who could save him from death, and he was heard because of his reverent submission." (Hebrews 5:7, NIV 1983)

SCRIPTURE REFERENCE	TEXT LOCATION IN BOOK	FULL CITATION
Hebrews 5:11-14	Chapter 3	"We have much to say about this, but it is hard to clarify it because you no longer try to understand. Though you ought to be teachers by this time, you need someone to teach you the elementary truths of God's word all over again. You need milk, not solid food! Being still an infant, anyone who lives on milk is not acquainted with the teaching about righteousness. But solid food is for the mature, who by constant use have trained themselves to distinguish good from evil." (Hebrews 5:11-14, NIV 1983)
Hebrews 6:10-12	Chapter 4	"God is not unjust; he will not forget your work and the love you have shown him as you have helped his people and continue to help them. We want each of you to show this same diligence to the very end, so that what you hope for may be fully realized. We do not want you to become lazy, but to imitate those who through faith and patience inherit what has been promised." (Hebrews 6:10-12, NIV 1983)

SCRIPTURE REFERENCE	TEXT LOCATION IN BOOK	FULL CITATION
Hebrews 10:24-25	Chapter 4	"And let us consider how we may spur one another on toward love and good deeds, not giving up meeting together, as some are in the habit of doing, but encouraging one another—and all the more as you see the Day approaching." (Hebrews 10:24-25, NIV 1983)
James 2:17	Chapter 4 Opening	"So too, faith, if it does not have works [to back it up], is by itself dead [inoperative and ineffective]." (James 2:17, Amplified Bible)
James 2:25-26	Chapter 2	"In the same way, was not even Rahab the prostitute considered righteous for what she did when she gave lodging to the spies and sent them off in a different direction? As the body without the spirit is dead, so faith without deeds is dead." (James 2:25-26, NIV 1983)
1 Peter 2:9	Tools & Resources	"But you are a chosen people, a royal priesthood, a holy nation, God's special possession, that you may declare the praises of him who called you out of darkness into his wonderful light." (1 Peter 2:9, NIV 1983)

PUBLISHED ARTICLES AND ONLINE SOURCES

SOURCE	CITATION	LOCATION IN BOOK
Crossroads Church Article	Patterson, Ali. "How a Hooker and Her Lies Pleased God." Crossroads Church. [Date and URL would need verification]	Chapter 2 - Rahab section

HISTORICAL SOURCES AND BIOGRAPHICAL INFORMATION

BIBLICAL WOMEN

FIGURE	PRIMARY SOURCE	SECONDARY SOURCES CONSULTED	LOCATION IN BOOK
Rahab	Joshua 2 (NIV 1983); Matthew 1:5 (NIV 1983); James 2:25-26 (NIV 1983); Hebrews 11:31 (NIV 1983)	Crossroads Church article by Ali Patterson	Chapter 2
Ruth	Book of Ruth (NIV 1983); Matthew 1:5 (NIV 1983)	Standard biblical commentaries	Chapter 2
Mary Magdalene	Luke 8:1-3 (NIV 1983); John 20:1-13 (NIV 1983)	Traditional church historical sources	Chapter 2

FIGURE	PRIMARY SOURCES	LOCATION IN BOOK
Martha Dandridge Washington	Mount Vernon Ladies' Association. "Martha Washington." Mount Vernon Official Website. https://www.mountvernon.org/george-washington/martha-washington/	Chapter 2
Sarah Breedlove (Madam C.J. Walker)	Bundles, A'Lelia. "On Her Own Ground: The Life and Times of Madam C.J. Walker." Scribner, 2001.	Chapter 2
	National Trust for Historic Preservation. "Madam C.J. Walker." https://savingplaces.org/places/madam-c-j-walker	Chapter 2

FIGURE	ORGANIZATION/PLATFORM	LOCATION IN BOOK
Aisha Oliver	Root2Fruit Chicago - Public website and social media presence	Chapter 4
Kristina Holloway	Faith On A Thousand - Public organization information	Chapter 4
Ebony Guerrier	Brown Bag Charity - Public charitable organization information	Chapter 4

BOOK AND RESOURCE RECOMMENDATIONS

BOOKS LISTED IN "TOOLS & RESOURCES" SECTION

TITLE	AUTHOR	PUBLISHER/YEAR
"Uninvited"	Lysa TerKeurst	Thomas Nelson, 2016
"Breaking Free"	Beth Moore	B&H Books, 2007
"The Purpose Driven Life"	Rick Warren	Zondervan, 2002
"Battlefield of the Mind"	Joyce Meyer	FaithWords, 2011
"The Gifts of Imperfection"	Brené Brown	Hazelden Publishing, 2010
"Healing the Shame That Binds You"	John Bradshaw	Health Communications, 2005
"Boundaries"	Henry Cloud and John Townsend	Zondervan, 2017
"Get Out of Your Head"	Jennie Allen	WaterBrook, 2020
"The Circle Maker"	Mark Batterson	Zondervan, 2011
"Anything"	Jennie Allen	Thomas Nelson, 2012
"Live Your Calling"	Kevin and Kay Marie Brennfleck	Jossey-Bass, 2008

PODCAST NAME	HOST/ORGANIZATION
"Therapy for Black Girls"	Dr. Joy Harden Bradford
"The Nicole Lapin Podcast"	Nicole Lapin
"Proverbs 31 Ministries Podcast"	Proverbs 31 Ministries
"The Dave Ramsey Show"	Dave Ramsey
"Joyce Meyer Enjoying Everyday Life"	Joyce Meyer Ministries

ADDITIONAL REFERENCES FOR VERIFICATION

ORGANIZATION	WEBSITE/CONTACT INFORMATION
MOPS (Mothers of Preschoolers)	https://www.mops.org/
She Reads Truth	https://shereadstruth.com/
Proverbs 31 Ministries	https://proverbs31.org/

NOTES FOR COMPLETE CITATION

FOR PUBLICATION, ADDITIONAL INFORMATION NEEDED:

1. **Contemporary Women**: Written permission from Aisha Oliver, Kristina Holloway, and Ebony Guerrier for inclusion of their stories and organizations
2. **Crossroads Church Article**: Full citation including publication date, author's full credentials, and URL
3. **Historical Sources**: Additional verification of historical facts from multiple academic sources
4. **Book Recommendations**: Current publication information and ISBN numbers for all recommended books

BIBLE TRANSLATION INFORMATION:

- Primary translation used: New International Version (NIV) 1983
- Secondary translation used: Amplified Bible (AMP) for James 2:17
- All biblical quotations should include copyright acknowledgment: "Scripture quotations taken from the HOLY BIBLE, NEW INTERNATIONAL VERSION® NIV® Copyright© 1973, 1978, 1984 by International Bible Society. Used by permission of Zondervan. All rights reserved."

COPYRIGHT ACKNOWLEDGMENTS REQUIRED:

- Scripture copyright acknowledgments for NIV 1983 and Amplified Bible
- Permission for any extended quotes from published books
- Attribution for historical information sources
- Permission statements from contemporary women featured

BIBLIOGRAPHY FORMAT FOR ACADEMIC/ PROFESSIONAL USE

- Bundles, A'Lelia. *On Her Own Ground: The Life and Times of Madam C.J. Walker*. New York: Scribner, 2001.
- Cloud, Henry, and John Townsend. *Boundaries: When to Say Yes, How to Say No to Take Control of Your Life*. Grand Rapids: Zondervan, 2017.
- Meyer, Joyce. *Battlefield of the Mind: Winning the Battle in Your Mind*. New York: FaithWords, 2011.
- Warren, Rick. *The Purpose Driven Life: What on Earth Am I Here For?* Grand Rapids: Zondervan, 2002.

- Patterson, Ali. "How a Hooker and Her Lies Pleased God." *Crossroads Church*. [Date and URL to be verified].

- *The Holy Bible, New International Version*. Grand Rapids: Zondervan, 1983.
- *The Amplified Bible*. Grand Rapids: Zondervan, 2015.

- Mount Vernon Ladies' Association. "Martha Washington." *Mount Vernon Official Website*. Accessed [Date]. https://www.mountvernon.org/george-washington/martha-washington/

- National Trust for Historic Preservation. "Madam C.J. Walker." *Saving Places*. Accessed [Date]. https://savingplaces.org/places/madam-c-j-walker

International Best Selling Author, Writer, Speaker, Podcast Host

Signature Podcast

Jori O'Neale is a highly sought-after speaker and trainer with 18+ years as an educator. She's the CEO and co-founder of IYH INNERTAINMENT LLC, a faith-based entertainment company building community through creative works. A 10-time published, 2-time best-selling author and publishing authority partner, Jori equips aspiring authors to turn life experiences into transformational books—without the overwhelm. After leaving a stable six-figure career to follow her God-given purpose, she now inspires others to stop settling and boldly share their stories.

"EMPOWERING PURPOSE-DRIVEN VOICES TO BE HEARD!"

Signature Topics
- The Power of Your Story
- Unleash Your God Given Gifts
- History Determines Herstory

Signature Workshops
- Your Story Matters
- Uncover Your God Given Gifts
- The Productive Christian: How to Go from Striving to Thriving

Companies Worked With

jorioneale@gmail.com   516-610-0250   @jorioneale

contact me to learn more: https://jorioneale.com

www.ingramcontent.com/pod-product-compliance
Lightning Source LLC
Chambersburg PA
CBHW070451090426
42735CB00012B/2508